SPANISH

FRESCOES

SPANISH FRESCOES

Of the Romanesque Period

INTRODUCTION BY

JUAN AINAUD

A MENTOR-UNESCO ART BOOK

PUBLISHED BY
THE NEW AMERICAN LIBRARY OF WORLD LITERATURE, INC.
BY ARRANGEMENT WITH UNESCO

Romanesque painting, which began to be re-evaluated for historical and iconographic reasons during the last century, has not until today been fully appreciated for the plastic qualities which, in our time, bring it within the area of our sensitivity and taste.

Historically speaking, awareness of Romanesque painting on the Iberian peninsula is first manifested in a few references made to it in the eighteenth century, but the study and understanding of Romanesque painting is very much more recent. There is, on the one hand, the monumental work on Catalan painting directed by J. Pijoan and published by the Institut d'Estudis Catalans from 1907 to 1921. On the other hand, a bibliography for Castile and León began with studies made by J. and R. Amador de los Ríos, M. Gómez-Moreno, P. Mata y Alvaro, J. Pérez Llamazares and J. Garnelo, while R. del Arco devoted himself to the art of Aragon. In addition to these studies, we have the research carried out by other scholars, both Spanish and foreign.

From 1906 on, the Museum of Barcelona, adopting a principle customary in other countries, began a systematic reproduction of all Catalan mural paintings. But in 1919 this work was abruptly halted and it was decided to remove the original works from the walls. The chief reason for this decision was that only by removing paintings as they were discovered could their slow and irreparable destruction be avoided. In countries like France, where

5

Church of St. Mary and St. Michael, Egara (Tarrassa).

Exterior view. Church of St. Clement, Tahull.

similar steps were not taken, there has been a steady disappearance, since the middle of the last century, of exceptional works of this kind.

The emergence of Romanesque art in Spain is very closely related to certain profound changes that took place within the internal structure of the country and in the form and meaning of its foreign affairs.

During the latter third of the tenth century there existed only one powerful state with a high cultural level, the Moslem Caliphate of Cordova. Within the Caliphate an important Christian segment developed, the Mozarabics, who were influenced by Arab culture but not converted to Islam and gravitated toward the small Christian kingdoms, especially those of Castile and León.

But the intolerance and the internal and external aggressiveness of Almanzor, Prime Minister to the Caliph Hixem II, destroyed the existing balance and the minimum conditions necessary for co-existence within the Caliphate, and provoked a series of violent attacks on the Christian populations to the north and north-east, culminating in the destruction of Barcelona (985) and Santiago de Compostela (997).

The reaction was not long in coming. The kingdoms and principalities which were attacked now made a tremendous internal effort to reorganize themselves quickly, and by 1010 their troops were prepared to fight, within Cordova itself, those battles which brought about the destruction of the Caliphate, and which completely overthrew it by 1032.

While the ancient Islamic kingdoms broke up into little states called "taifas," the old and independent centers within the Christian territories spread out and became stronger: the kingdom of León was joined with Asturias and Galicia; the so-called empire of Sancho the Great of Navarre (1000-1035) included, in addition to Navarre, the counties of Castile, Aragon, Sobrarbe and Ribagorza, made into kingdoms after the death of Sancho the Great. Ribagorza was the only Catalan territory separated from the rest of Catalonia, which came under the hegemony of the Count of Barcelona.

8

It was in this period that normal relations between Christian Spain and the rest of Europe were established and began to develop.

Before or shortly after the foundations of Cluny and Moissac, and as a result of direct action taken by the Pontifical legates, religious and monastic orders from France and Italy established centers in Spain. These orders united the local centers with those in France and Italy: San Martino of Albenga, San Michele della Chiusa, St. Victor of Marseilles, St. Pons of Thomières, as well as the Premonstratensians, the Augustinian canons, the Cistercians, and the great military orders of Palestinian origin — the Knights Templar and the Hospitalers — with those of Spanish origin: Montesa, Santiago, Alcántara, Calatrava, all of them having widely differing characteristics. The great richness and variety of these influences and their constantly changing character are decisive factors when we try to explain the many-sided artistic panorama that existed in Spain during the eleventh and twelfth centuries.

The various surviving classical forms found expression also in the beginnings of Spanish medieval painting. Thus, in some of the most ancient churches built by the kings of Aragon, for example the church of Santullano (812-842), we find painted on its walls certain architectural motifs resembling those from the eastern Mediterranean coast. And the ancient bishopric of Egara, situated on the western coast of the Iberian peninsula, is endowed with three churches whose naturalistic decoration, with landscapes in the background, can be related to other European works of the second half of the ninth century.

We must mention, if only briefly, the magnificent school of Mozarabic painting, which contrasted with the traditions of the ancient world and which evolved during the tenth century. Unfortunately, except for the small traces found in a few Asturian churches and the Catalonian church of Campdévanol (the church has been destroyed), the only examples we have of this art are found in illuminated manuscripts. These illuminations, however, are frequently of high quality and splendid coloring and afford the

Interior, Church of St. Clement, Tahull.

Interior, the King's Pantheon, Collegiate Church of St. Isidore, León

student some idea of what the characteristics of Mozarabic painting may have been.

Other scattered works, of a rough character, seem to testify in certain cases to the art of local artists who, even with limited means, were able to produce works of great expressive power. As an example, we have the paintings found in the pre-Romanesque church of Pedret (Plate 1), to the north of Barcelona, which were later painted over in a different style of Romanesque art.

It is not until the eleventh century, however, that the arrival of new elements and their subsequent modification and developement by Spanish painters made possible the evolution of those characteristics which can be properly termed Spanish Romanesque.

Romanesque painting has survived almost solely in religious buildings, which, however, sometimes provide examples of contemporaneous secular themes. Mural painting was done mainly in the apses, but in many churches the interior walls must have been entirely covered with painted decorations. Occasionally, sheltered exterior areas, such as porticos, were also painted. The wooden altars, statuary, and furniture were very often painted over with brilliant colors. There remain in Catalonia many altar frontals which sometimes had lateral panels added, although these latter pieces survived less frequently. There also exist wooden crosses painted both front and back, most frequently with an image of the crucified Christ, although other popular images, such as the head of Christ and the Virgin and Child often appear worked into a decorative scheme covering the Cross. In the more complex designs, scenes of Calvary, the Descent from the Cross, and even images of saints may be seen.

The images in these churches are usually grouped around the majestic figure of the Almighty, who is replaced, in churches where there is a special veneration for the Virgin Mary, by the Epiphany or the Adoration of the Magi. In these cases, God reigns from his mother's knees, the living throne of Jesus. These visions of the Divinity are most often painted either on the upper vaults or half cupolas in the apse — with their surface and shape related to the celestial vault — or in the center of the altarpieces.

This early phase of Romanesque painting is characterized by powerful expressionism and a dynamic freedom of composition. The altarpiece dedicated to the Saints Quirico and Julita, found in their own chapel in Durro (Plate 3), is an example of this period, which seems to have survived longest in the area of the Pyrenees.

Not far from Durro, the Boí murals (Plate 2), with their elongated and highly expressive human forms, are closely related to the Durro altarpiece; but in contrast with the vivid hues (greens, yellows, intense reds) of the latter, those of Boí are painted in pale shades of gray, ochre, and scarlet, and reveal an art which is more monumental and refined.

Probably soon after this, the work of other painters first appeared around Gerona and then moved southward. The scenes from Genesis and the Apostles in the church of Osormort (Vich Episcopal Museum) are attributed to the best known of these artists, the Master of Osormort. Also attributed to this painter are those paintings in the small church of Marenyá, which depict St. Stephen, and those of El Brull (Vich Episcopal Museum), which also picture scenes from Genesis and from the infancy of Jesus. These figures are usually quite small, with great variety in arrangement and attitudes; the master's palette is mainly made up of ochres, earth-tones and bluish-grays. What stands out are the enormous eyes, the shape of the heads, with the hair generally swept back. The closest parallel we have to these works is the paintings found in the crypt of St. Savin-sur-Gartempe, and in the miniatures that decorate a manuscript recounting the life of St. Radegunda at Poitiers, both of which date from the end of the eleventh century. The architecture of the churches in which the paintings are found also suggests this chronology. However, even the architectural evidence for dating is unsupported by documents except in one case: we know that El Brull was consecrated in 1062. In the final analysis the chronology must rest on our knowledge of styles in the painting.

Artajona. Saints. Detail from the Last Judgement murals.
Pamplona Museum.

14

Tower, Collegiate Church of St. Isidore, León.

Six years later the church of Sescorts was consecrated and in it there are scenes from the story of Adam and Eve (Vich Episcopal Museum). Following the Sescorts style but belonging to a more southern school are the churches of Polinyá (consecrated in 1122) and Barbará, which was probably consecrated between 1116 and 1137 by the bishop St. Oleguer. Their stylistic similarities provide the decisive reason for placing all of this group of works in the first third of the twelfth century (Plate 4). Parallel with this, a group of churches were decorated in Roussillon, the best known of which are those of La Clusa and Fenollar. The latter is pre-Romanesque in style, and its walls must have been painted around 1100, with scenes from the life of Christ and a vast apocalyptical composition, both attributed to one painter.

During the first quarter of the twelfth century, a painter, popular in character, reveals a great personal and expressive power in the paintings he did on the lateral walls and complementary areas of the two churches in Tahull (Plates 6 and 7), consecrated in 1123. His use of simple colors, ochres, earth-tones, grays, easily obtainable in the locality, did not constitute an obstacle to creating paintings as expressive as that of the fight between David and Goliath (Plate 10), found in the church of St. Mary (Art Museum of Catalonia, Barcelona).

The abundance of works produced — and preserved — in Catalonia makes it possible to study, perhaps as in no other part of Europe, the simultaneous labors of several great masters having extremely different artistic origins, and beside them or following them a galaxy of minor artists.

Among the minor artists, we can identify the work associated witn certain well-known names: the Master of Pedret, who reflects the Hellenistic tradition, most probably inspired by Italian models (jeweled crowns, Grecian frets, double-hooked folds), and who, not scorning portraits, paints with a personal interpretation of perspective; the Master of Mur, who did the baldachin of Ribes, the frontal of Hix, and a few other works, all of which have in common a wise use of plane geometry combined with splendid colors; the two painters responsible for the apses of Tahull, St. Clement's, and St. Mary's; and various other artists active in the dioceses of Vich, Gerona, and Barcelona, as well as some exceptional specialists in painting on wood, first-rate examples of which are found in Solsona, Vich, Gerona, and Barcelona.

The influences of their art can often be traced beyond the works painted by the minor masters previously mentioned. For example, those of Sorpe and St. Coloma borrowed elements from the Master of Pedret, and these works are found respectively in the churches of Pallars and Andorra; the artist of Sorpe also painted the apse of St. Mary of Tahull. The consecration, in 1163, of the church of St. Romá dels Bons, in Andorra, one of the churches known to be painted by the Master of St. Coloma, gives some indication of the chronology of his activity.

We should not forget, on the other hand, an important group of paintings which still exist in Roussillon, Vallespir, Conflent and Cerdaña — Catalan districts which were to be separated — wholly or in part — from the rest of Catalonia in 1659 by the Treaty of the Pyrenees. All the various stages and characteristics are represented by interesting works from the most archaic styles to the most highly developed (Serrabona, Sureda, Arles — dated 1157 — Estavar, etc.), including the last stages, which will be discussed later on.

It is interesting to note the spread of the art of certain masters beyond the Catalan districts, and this must have taken many diverse forms, if we judge by the examples which have survived.

In the paintings in Vals, in Ariège, the result is a local reflection of another artist's work, in this case the Master of Pedret. This deduction is made plausible by the fact that he worked in the valley of Arán which, like Vals, belonged during the Middle Ages to the Diocese of Comminges.

The extraordinary Master of St. Clement of Tahull decorated a small apse in the cathedral at Roda, to which the valley of Boí belonged until 1140; it was its bishop,

St. Ramón, who in 1123 consecrated the two churches of Tahull.

The personal action of this same prelate can help us to explain the activity of the Master of St. Mary in very distant places: Berlanga, Maderuelo (Prado Museum), and perhaps Tubilla del Agua, Castilian territories which, between 1111-1134 were under the direct rule of the king of Aragon, Alfonso the Warrior. The latter was closely associated with St. Ramón, who accompanied him on his military expeditions, and aided in the repopulation of areas in Castile, largely with people from the region of the Pyrenees.

Apart from this are the magnificent paintings in the Collegiate Church of St. Isidore, the result of the munificence of Ferdinand II of León (1157-1188), who with his wife Urraca appears in a portait among these paintings, and the valuable but damaged fragments of the murals in the apse of St. Pelayo of Perazancas.

The León paintings are found in the Pantheon of the Kings, a dome-covered portico facing the western side of the church. On the domes — apparently covering older paintings — there are vast compositions with complex historical and symbolic themes. The most attractive of these is the *Annunciation to the Shepherds* (Plate 13), with its multitude of anecdotal details and its human and decorative significance.

In the last years of the twelfth century, paralleling the deterioration of the traditional forms of the previous age, there appear in Spain certain exceptionally fine examples of a new European pictorial style, characterized by a strong Byzantine influence. Nevertheless, and in spite of the fact that this remote tie with Byzantium is undeniable, the resulting stylistic changes in Spain are very complex, and certain echoes — and not those of least importance — seem rather to relate directly to England.

Among the paintings which show the effects of the influx of the new European style into Spain, the group to which we may attribute the earliest date is that of various paintings on panels which come from Cardana, or bordering areas. These include the Valltarga frontal

León. Second half of twelfth century. Detail from the Annunciation to the Shepherds. Collegiate Church of St. Isidore.

(Plate 20) now in the Art Museum of Catalonia, Barcelona, and, from Orellá, the fragment of a baldachin. A miniature from the year 1195, from the monastery of St. Martin of Canigou, is partially inspired by this group and helps to place it chronologically. These are paintings with an intense Italo-Byzantine character, with excellent drawing and brilliant and subtle coloring.

At about the same time, two other painters, the Masters of Lluçá and Aviá, began to work in Catalonia in a new style but one which was much more Romanesque in the traditional sense. The quality of their colors is very rich but lighter than that of the previous group. To the group of the Master of Lluçá we owe paintings on panels, including a cross and three altarpieces in Lluçá, which gave him his name, the mural paintings at Puigreig and those from St. Paul of Casserres, now in the Archeological Museum of the Diocese, Solsona (Plates 22 and 23). The Master of Aviá derives his name from the frontal from the church of St. Mary of Aviá (Art Museum of Catalonia, Barcelona) with the beautiful *Nativity* (Plate 21), very well executed. Other works by his hand are the frontals of Rotgés and St. Peter of Ribesaltes, in Bergadá and Roussilon. His art is reflected — unfortunately with little talent — in the work of a minor painter called the Master of Vidrá.

There were, of course, other painters who followed the western traditions more exclusively, as did the painter of the frontal of Mosoll and the Master of Espinelves (Plates 16 and 17) who, around 1200, painted a frontal —which comes from the place in the diocese of which gives him his name — as well as the murals in the apse of St. Mary of Egara, dedicated to St. Thomas à Becket. Other paintings from the same period were found in the western part of Catalonia. Some are traditional, like the *Last Supper* in the Vich Episcopal Museum (Plate 26) and episodes in the life of St. Catherine, in Seo d'Urgell; others show a greater Byzantine influence: the frontal in the Art Museum of Catalonia, Barcelona, the cross in the Museum of Archeology in Madrid, and the mural paintings of St. Stephen in Andorra La Vella, with scenes of the Passion and other episodes. Farther to the southeast, the important group of frontals and other pieces with painted decorations and backgrounds of stucco in relief, to which the frontal of Chiá (Art Museum of Catalonia, Barcelona) belongs, were dedicated to St. Martin of Tours and signed *Johannes pintor* (Plate 24). This series, valuable within its popular flavor, must have been in progress until the middle of the thirteenth century and perhaps even later.

In Ribagorza, the paintings in the crypt or lower room built under the small apse of the pulpit in the Cathedral of Roda show a popular style from the second half of the twelfth century on, while in the Aragonese church of St. John in Uncastillo interesting fragments of a more sophisticated art can probably be dated around 1200. The frontal of Gesera, dedicated to St. John the Baptist (Plate 25), the frontal of Liesa, with scenes from the life of St. Vincent, and the upper (and oldest) section of the murals of St. Fructuoso of Bierge constitute a nucleus of art in the Aragonese Pyrenees of a later date and, although crude, it is very expressive.

In contrast with all of this are the magnificent paintings in the chapel of the monastery of Sijena. More than their mutilated fragments, badly damaged by fire in 1936, the personal recollections and the abundant photographic documentation dating from before the fire allow us to appreciate their exceptional quality. On the arches and walls there is a double row of busts representing the genealogy of Jesus and scenes from the Old and New Testament, which are completed around the arches by flowers and fantastic animals. The dominant colors are ochre, salmon-pink and sky-blue, found nowhere else in Spanish mural painting, and still visible in a small sample which remains intact. This example corroborates the similarities of style and iconography which compel us to accept the theory that there is a direct link between this work and the art of the Winchester Bible, the so-called "Morgan Page", the stained-glass windows of the genealogy of Christ in Canterbury Cathedral and old English manuscripts which English historians date around the last years of the twelfth century. A chronicler of cenobite life, the prior Moreno, affirms that the paintings of the genealogy of Jesus at Sijena were done in 1232, which differs to a certain extent from the accepted chronology for the above-mentioned English works, but it corresponds perfectly with another date, that of 1258, at which time the monastery church was consecrated. The church was then completely painted and in the apse there still exist works from the brush of a disciple or direct follower of the Master who did the capitulary room.

Gudiol suggests that this second artist was also the principal or sole painter of a series of murals from Artajona, Olite, and Artaiz which are conserved in the Pamplona Museum.

In Castile we know of only example of a quality and period similar to those of the Sijena paintings, namely the fragments of murals, decorated with large animal themes, coming from a room in the monastery of St. Peter of Arlanza (Burgos). Farther to the west, we have an excellent echo in the miniature portrait of Alfonso IX (1188-1230) on horseback with a huge heraldic lion, mentioned in Cartulary A of the Cathedral of Santiago de Compostela. Its date tends to confirm the global chronology of the style. The lion frescos of the thirteenth century which are most interesting are those of the capitulary room of St. Isidore, now called the Chapel of the Quiñones. These are within the normal Romanesque tradition.

The fragment of a painting that is perhaps earlier, but in any case of uncertain date, represents a vision of God with figures of saints and a bishop in the apse of the church of Christ of Light in Toledo. In this same city, the church of St. Román still possesses a very substantial part of its mural paintings, dated around 1221, in which Moorish elements are juxtaposed with more or less Byzantine-Christian ones.

Paintings on panels are very scarce in Castile and León. We know nevertheless some interesting examples: a slim figure of St. Paul in the Episcopal Museum of Ávila, and a wooden chest with the images of the twelve Apostles

Aviá. Circa 1200. Virgin and Child. Detail from frontal in the Church of St. Mary. Art Museum of Catalonia, Barcelona.

and figures from the life of Christ in the Cathedral of Astorga.

Worthy of note, before the full development of Gothic art, is a group of thirteenth century paintings in Barcelona, the style of which, moreover, was introduced into the island of Majorca, a new area for the study of Romanesque art. In Barcelona, we know from this period the decorations in the ancient Royal Palace with parades of horsemen and soldiers; fragments from an aristocratic house in the Calle de Durán y Bas, with horsemen, animals and heraldic themes, as well as flowers and geometric patterns; and the evocative scenes of the conquest of Majorca by James I in 1229, found at No. 15, Calle Montcada, and which are set off by an equally richly painted wooden ceiling. In Palma Majorca, two important paintings on wood exist in a similar style.

Some very attractive paintings, by the so-called Master of Soriguerola (Plates 27 and 28), in the districts to the north of Catalonia, show a step toward Gothic art in ornamental elements and other details, although in basic style they still remain within those Romanesque traditions so characteristic of this region.

ILLUSTRATIONS

1

4

7

ATM

ATEV

8

11

13

ꟸⳑRꟸꟾℒꟾⳑℒⱱⱣℒ𝒞𝒞ℒꟾꟾℒꟾⱣ

OLYMPIS MEGARICA

CRNIFI CES

19

MARIA

24

28

BIBLIOGRAPHY

The following is a summary general bibliography. More extensive bibliographies, totalling over 150 references in all, are given in the works of Post, Gudiol i Cunill, Durliat and Ainaud mentioned below.

J. PIJOAN, Les pintures murals catalanes, Barcelona, Institut d'Estudis Catalans, 1907-1921.

M. GÓMEZ MORENO, Catálogo monumental de España, Provincia de León (1906-1908), Madrid, 2 Vols., 1925.

J. GUDIOL i CUNILL, La pintura migeval catalana, Els Primitius, Barcelona, S. Babrar, Vols. I-III, 1927-1955.

C. R. POST, A History of Spanish Painting, Cambridge (Mass.), Harvard University Press, Vols. I-XII, 1930-1959.

W. W. S. COOK and J. GUDIOL RICART, "Pintura e Imaginería románicas", Ars Hispaniae, Vol. VI, Madrid, 1950.

M. DURLIAT, Arts anciens du Roussillon - Peinture, Perpignan, 1954.

J. FOLCH i TORRES, La pintura románica sobre fusta, Monumenta Cataloniae IX, Barcelona, Alpha, 1956.

J. AINAUD and W. W. S. COOK, Spain - Romanesque Paintings, Unesco World Art Series, 1957.

A. GRABAR and C. NORDENFALK, La peinture romane, Geneva, Skira, 1953.

L. SCHREYER, Romanische Malerei, Bonn, Adamas, 1959.

E. JUNYENT, Catalogne romane, Vols. I-II, La Pierre-qui-vire, Zodiaque, 1960-1961.

CONTENTS

CONTENTS

Continued on next page ▶

CONTENTS

CONTENTS

CONTENTS

Continued on next page ▶

BIBLIOGRAPHY

The following is a summary general bibliography. More extensive bibliographies, totalling over 150 references in all, are given in the works of Post, Gudiol i Cunill, Durliat and Ainaud mentioned below.

J. PIJOAN, *Les pintures murals catalanes*, Barcelona, Institut d'Estudis Catalans, 1907-1921.

M. GÓMEZ MORENO, *Catálogo monumental de España, Provincia de León* (1906-1908), Madrid, 2 Vols., 1925.

J. GUDIOL i CUNILL, *La pintura migeval catalana, Els Primitius*, Barcelona, S. Babrar, Vols. I-III, 1927-1955.

C. R. POST, *A History of Spanish Painting*, Cambridge (Mass.), Harvard University Press, Vols. I-XII, 1930-1959.

W. W. S. COOK and J. GUDIOL RICART, "Pintura e Imaginería románicas", *Ars Hispaniae*, Vol. VI, Madrid, 1950.

M. DURLIAT, *Arts anciens du Roussillon - Peinture*, Perpignan, 1954.

J. FOLCH i TORRES, *La pintura románica sobre fusta, Monumenta Cataloniae* IX, Barcelona, Alpha, 1956.

J. AINAUD and W. W. S. COOK, *Spain - Romanesque Paintings*, Unesco World Art Series, 1957.

A. GRABAR and C. NORDENFALK, *La peinture romane*, Geneva, Skira, 1953.

L. SCHREYER, *Romanische Malerei*, Bonn, Adamas, 1959.

E. JUNYENT, *Catalogne romane*, Vols. I-II, La Pierre-qui-vire, Zodiaque, 1960-1961.

CONTENTS